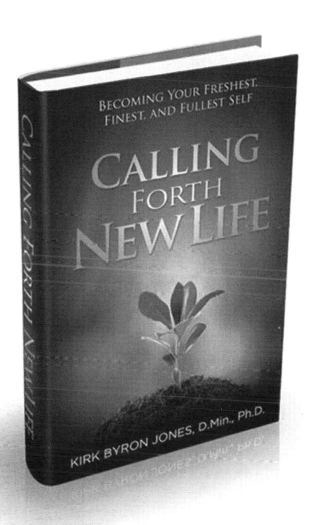

BECOMING YOUR FRESHEST,
FINEST, AND FULLEST SELF

CALLING
FORTH
NEW LIFE

KIRK BYRON JONES, D.Min., Ph.D.

Now when He ad said these things, He cried with a loud voice,

"Lazarus, come forth!"

--John 11:43

PRAISE
for
CALLING FORTH NEW LIFE

The writings of Dr. Kirk Byron Jones have become constant companions to me on this life journey. This latest gift, *Calling Forth New Life*, is no exception. In a world wrought with burdens, Kirk Byron Jones challenges us to pay attention to the weight we place on our faith, and to make a decision to enjoy our journey. I am deeply grateful for the gentle reminders disbursed throughout this deeply thoughtful meditation to stop, receive God's grace, and be replenished. You will not be disappointed that you have chosen *Calling Forth New Life* as a companion piece for your journey.

--**Traci D. Blackmon**, *Executive Minister of Justice & Witness, The United Church of Christ*

In his book, *Calling Forth New Life*, Kirk Byron Jones does a magnificent job of showing that the Bible and the Law of Attraction are not mutually exclusive and do not contradict each other. Dr. Jones has created a beautiful bridge of understanding, regardless of whether you consider yourself religious or spiritual. I highly recommend it!

-- **Eva Gregory**, author of *The Feel Good Guide to Prosperity* and *Life Lessons for Mastering the Law of Attraction* co-authored with **Jack Canfield**

Reading Dr. Kirk Jones's 'Calling Forth New Life' is like sipping water from a deep well on a hot North Carolina August day! Drawing from a wide range of inspirational sources from childhood memories to Jazz to ecstatic poetry from Hafiz, Jones reminds us all of the refreshing tones of the sacred inner voice that brings clarity and creativity, giving rise to the divine imagination in all of us. His latest edition to his body of work firmly establishes him as a key pastoral voice for those of us on the frontlines of social change.

    --Jeffrey L. Brown, President, National RECAP Group

Release your creativity and transform your life with uplifting words and innovative practices found in *Calling Forth New Life: Becoming Your Freshest, Finest, and Fullest Self* by Kirk Byron Jones. Jones' books fuel my soul, and this one is taking me to the next level as it encourages me to break free from a self-imposed prison. Can you imagine opening the prison door and walking out to embrace transformation, becoming a "co-conspirator with God" where creativity and new opportunities overflow?

    --Cal Shook, Writer/Photographer

Years ago I took a course that Jones taught called *'Pastor, Prophet, Priest: Will the real Preacher Stand Up?'* In so many ways this book robes itself in each of those holy offices. Like many of his other texts, this one fell into my lap at just the right time and God has used it to help 'Call Forth' a new season of ministry in my life. It will most certainly play a similar role in your journey."

    --Charles L. Howard, Ph.D., University Chaplain, University of Pennsylvania

This book stirred my inner being to new life! What an engaging, enlightening, and empowering tool for Bible study, book clubs and discussion forums for men, women and youth groups. From the first page to the last page, you will not want to put this book down. I am definitely adding to the Divas for Christ's book club.

   --Altonnette D. Hawkins, D. Min., Founder, Take Care With Self Care Center

Jones' fresh theological language provokes joy with jazzy phrases such as: *patient enthusiasm, enflamed attitude, sacred esteem, actively determined, and Fiercely Free Spirit.* But he doesn't leave you floundering with empty words. Dr. Jones provides direction with spiritual practices that will open your heart to the redemptive living and resurrection joy. You owe this powerful read to yourself and to the world so that you can become your freshest, finest and fullest self!

   --Mark Seifried, *Transitional Ministry Specialist, United Church of Christ*

Calling Forth New Life captured the attention of every surviving cell in my body, mind, and soul. Dr. Jones has a way of sounding alarms that can only result in a change. What a breathtaking and brilliant book that will touch and change your perspective on life. READ IT and ABSORB!!!

   --Wilma Randolph, D.Min., Senior Pastor, New Prospect Baptist Church and Author of *Unspeakable Joy*

Drawing from a deep well of prayer and practice, Kirk Byron Jones brings forth living water of wisdom and inspiration. When I opened

Calling Forth New Life, I was feeling discouraged. But discouragement and Kirk Byron Jones cannot long abide in the same place. My discouragement fled, replaced by gratitude and serenity.

    --Fred Small, President, Creation Coalition

The pulpit, the pew, families, and communities are being plummeted with the languages, images and realities of death, despair, hopelessness, and negativity. Kirk Byron Jones presents his prophetic and pastoral concerns, and weaves them with scripture, hope, practical suggestions and humor to argue the necessity for transformed life. After reading *Calling Forth New Life*, I feel like I am drowning in God's love.

    --Muriel L. Johnson, Regional Associate Minister, American Baptist Churches of the Great Rivers Region

Dr. Kirk Byron Jones does it again with his latest book, *Calling Forth New Life: Becoming Your Freshest, Finest, and Fullest Self.* With the age old gospel story of Jesus' raising of Lazarus as his back drop, Dr. Jones reminds us that the journey to our freshest, finest, and fullest selves is something that is called forth with intention and nurtured with grace and gratitude. This book is a must read for those on a personal path to healing and wholeness.

    --Mia J. Douglas, Director of Discipleship, Asylum Hill Congregational Church, UCC - Hartford, CT

In *Calling Forth New Life*, Kirk Bryon Jones reminds us to reposition ourselves and be open to change and transformation with reflective tools to guide us there.

--**Deidre Hill Butler**, Ph.D., Associate Professor of Sociology and Director of Africana Studies, Union College Schenectady, New York

Given the present state of our world and the increasing issues that impact us individually and corporately, *Calling Forth New Life: Becoming Your Freshest, Finest, and Fullest Self* presents itself at a "kairos moment." Kirk Byron Jones investigates familiar passages from our sacred text and couples them with life illustrations to introduce us to principles necessary to call forth new life.

While God is the source of life, we can apply these principles so that we may be a conduit for new life in our individual lives and the world around us. No matter where you are on your growth journey, *Calling Forth New Life* presents principles that will help you reach the next milestone or as Jones puts it, "level up."

-- **Eva Melton Billingsley**, MAR Minister and Community Advocate

Calling Forth New Life

BECOMING YOUR FRESHEST, FINEST, AND FULLEST SELF

Dr. Kirk Byron Jones

Soaring Spirit Press
Randolph, Massachusetts
ISBN: 0692535365
ISBN 13: 9780692535363

To the Lively, Lighthearted, and Loving Saints of Zion Baptist Church

in Lynn, Massachusetts.

Eternal Gratitude for Calling Forth Pastoral New Life in Me!

Gratitude Inspires Attitude.

An Inspired Attitude Enhances Perception.

An Enhanced Perception Unleashes New Possibilities.

Contents

The Divine Persistence of New Life

§

"I am come that you might have life, and that you might have it more abundantly."

--John 10:10

ONCE, I DROVE UP TO a business and noticed a memorial of flowers and stuffed animals around a large light pole. I asked the proprietor what had happened, and he told me of a terrible accident involving a police pursuit and the deaths of two persons. He spoke slowly and sadly, and then told me that the light pole turned loving memorial was brand new. The pole it replaced was broken in half with the impact of the car.

We live in a time when we see immediately, regularly, and vividly life broken. At the moment of this writing, tragedies in Nepal, Baltimore, and Charleston, South Carolina bring us horrid images of life suddenly snuffed out or snatched away.

Yet, as heartbreaking as these and other tragedies are, the picture of death is never the last one we see. In tragedy after tragedy, signs of new life appear in the hope and devotion of survivors to keep on keeping on, no matter what. Though repeatedly assailed, life is undeniably resilient. The tender memorial at the foot of the new light pole is a sign of the divine persistence of life.

There is a power in the universe that is as tenacious as death can be heartless. It is the divine power of new life that insists on having the last word, no matter what. Indeed, a heartache is still a life sign.

Nowhere is such divine power better evidenced than in the revolutionary new life vitality of Jesus. He who was brought back to life, lived, breathed, preached, and called forth new life:

Jesus said to her, "Did I not say to you that if you would believe you would see the glory of God?" Then they took away the stone from the place where the dead man was lying. And Jesus lifted up His eyes and said, "Father, I thank You that You have heard Me. And I know that You always hear Me, but because of the people who are standing by I said this, that they may believe that You sent Me." Now when He had said these things, He cried with a loud voice, "Lazarus, come forth!" And he who had died came out bound hand and foot with grave clothes, and his face was wrapped with a cloth. Jesus said to them, "Loose him, and let him go."

(John 11:41-44)

What if the power for bringing forth new life was available to us today?

What if we could call forth new life not just for the benefit of personal well-being but to the best blessing of our relationships, organizations, and communities?

What if we were able to imagine and create in a New Life Spirit, personal attitudes and behaviors leading to new social structures and policies previously deemed impossible, or never ever dreamed before?

Keep the "What ifs" in mind as we take a closer look at how Jesus was able to call forth new life.

As you revisit this wondrous biblical story, or hear it for the first time, I hope that you are inspired to call forth new life right where you are, and become enthralled with the life of daily transformation. Note those areas in your life in which you long for transformation. Begin to imagine regularly and specifically how things may be different in a relationship, on your job, in a beloved organization, and in your community. Link your dreams and desires to the new life dispositions and methods you are about to discover. I dare you.

Going forth, I wish for you curious anticipation, joyful satisfaction, and patient enthusiasm. Concerning the latter, though genuine change can sometimes happen in an instant, most of the time transformation takes time. The words of Henri Nouwen offer profound guidance:

> *A gentle person treads lightly, listens* carefully, *looks tenderly, and touches with reverence. A gentle person knows that true growth requires nurture not force.*

Inside the gift of new life is the gift of being gentle with yourself, others, and life itself.

> *Jesus did not force new life upon Lazarus; Jesus called forth new life.*

CHAPTER 1

Gratitude Inspires Attitude

§

"Gratitude grows new life!"

HEARING VOICES

JESUS HEARD MANY VOICES THE days leading up to, and on the day he raised Lazarus from the dead.

John 11:8 reveals that he heard the voices of disciples who tried to discourage him from returning to a place where an attempt had been made on his life. Note that it is not one of the golden ones, Peter, James, or John, that speaks up for going with Jesus, even if it means going back to the valley of the shadow of death. It is Thomas' voice that we hear. We often refer to him as "Doubting Thomas" for not readily believing in the risen Lord, but he is the one wearing the courage here. Indeed, his lighthearted manner of engaging the challenge turned out to be just the right words at the right time. "Let us go, that we might die with Him," Thomas said. (John 11:16) There was just enough joke in his words to jolt the other disciples out of their fearful hesitation.

When Jesus did arrive on the scene, he heard the voices of two sisters, Martha and Mary. They spoke with broken hearts about their brother's untimely death, and a friend's unforgivable delay. How disheartening it must have been for Jesus to have his friend's demise tied to his tardiness. Jesus heard the same sorrowful accusation from each sister at two different times: "If you had been here, my brother would not have died." (John 11:22, 32)

Next, there were voices of the villagers murmuring amongst themselves as to why the alleged miracle worker wasn't around to work a miracle for his so-called friend. (John 11:37)

Though the voices and emotions were heavy that day, Jesus is able to hear them without letting them halt him. Moreover, he turned to his inner voice in order to address the Sacred Voice that had called him to his work of unleashing the sacred potential in others.

"Father, I thank You that You have heard Me. And I know that You always hear Me."

Amid the voices of discouragement, dismay, and disdain, Jesus remains faithful to his own inner sacred voice. Of the immense value of our own inner voices, Howard Thurman once said, "There is something in every one of you that waits and listens for the sound of the genuine in yourself....And if you cannot hear it, you will all of your life spend your days on the ends of strings that somebody else pulls."

Jesus used his inner sacred voice to pray, and to affirm that in spite of all else that he had heard and would hear, God heard him and would continue to do so.

If you can trust that God hears you, you can make it, no matter what else you hear.

Unleashing the Vital Energy of Gratitude

Jesus expresses gratitude, not *after* the miracle but *before* the miracle: "Father, I thank you that You have heard me."

To call forth new life in any situation, begin with gratitude. Start with being thankful for what is.

The gratitude I speak of is more than a hollow obligatory expression of thanks. As important as that is, I am speaking about an earnest feeling of appreciation so potent that it lifts the spirit, and so pervasive, that there is no room left for negative sentiments.

This is the secret power of gratitude: True thankfulness cannot abide with negative feelings.

Authentic gratitude makes negativity so uncomfortable it has to excuse itself.

Because it is undiluted by negativity, genuine gratitude carries the pure energy of vibrant and vital life, and is capable of overcoming negative feelings that suppress life. The Lazarus resurrection narrative illustrates this as we see Jesus moving beyond the negative judgments in the air that were against him, and with the positive winds of gratitude lifting him and carrying him onward and upward.

Gratitude was the game-changer.

Had Jesus only listened and allowed himself to be influenced by the voices that questioned his compassion and concern, he may have been emotionally crushed, and Lazarus would have remained dead.

There is no raising of Lazarus from the grave, apart from Jesus raising his voice in gratitude.

Whenever we speak gratitude to the grave, the ground shakes with new life.

Gratitude opens the way for us to dream and do with a beyond-the-sky-is-the-limit mind-set.

Gratitude keeps the channel open for God's resurrection power to flow freely and fully through us.

Gratitude clears the airways of all the sediment and stress that can hinder the vibrant new life power that is in the air all the time. Because God never stops being God, new life is always in the air.

Gratitude grows new life!

Be Grateful for You

When was last time you were truly thankful for you? You are a unique expression of God's loving creativity. You are wondrous as you are, prior to any improvements. In an attempt to match a socially constructed image of perfection, we often miss the precious value of who we are as our genuine selves. Start practicing self-appreciation by opening the gift of being gentle with yourself. Take time for the things that satisfy you from the inside out. Notice what drains you and what energizes you, and spend far more time with the latter. Spend more than sufficient amounts of time to rest, to be at peace, to wander and wonder, to grieve and heal—to feel God's all-abiding grace through it all.

If for a moment you should feel guilty about focusing such attention on yourself, and suspect that it is selfish; think again. Just the opposite is selfish. By chronically ignoring ourselves, we risk the world never seeing our freshest, fullest, and finest manifestation in the world. Self-care is an act of great benevolence, not selfishness. You, at you your best, is the best offering you have to give to the world. If you need a good example of how powerful such an offering can be, note that before Jesus raised Lazarus from the dead, he took two days off. (John 11:6) Jesus was able to give new life because he had new life in him to give.

Before Jesus blessed Lazarus with restoration, he blessed himself with restoration.

THE DEAD CAN'T CALL FORTH NEW LIFE

One morning, I sat feeling drained and tired. I felt as if I had given all I had to church and community, and I had nothing left to give. Indeed, it was worse than that. My skin seemed to ache from all the pulls and tugs from persons, needs, and obligations for my time and attention. I was sick from giving. That's when I made the greatest discovery of all during my pastoral career: *My first job is not to give anything to anybody. My first job is to receive the soul restorative and replenishing grace of God's precious love each day, several times a day.*

From that new life moment on, imagining receiving God's love in such a way as to actually feel beloved became an integral part of my daily devotional times. My favorite spiritual visualization is to see myself floating on the soothing waters of God's unconditional love.

The undoing of much of our work whether it be ministry, community organizing, or something else, is laboring from a space of chronic emptiness. As a result we are unable to generate fresh critical analysis and creative ideas our world longs for. We are simply too stressed to be fresh and too deadened to be dynamic.

Deadened spirits cannot call forth new life. It will take enlivened spirits to enliven our world.

Jesus rested two days before engaging the resurrection challenge. He paused. The pause is what made the power possible. Wayne Muller expresses it this way: *Our most creative inspirations and epiphanies often arise when we finally stop looking for them, when we let go our pushing, seeking, and striving.*

I had such a moment some years ago while standing in the refurbished den of one of the homes I'd grown up in New Orleans, Louisiana. Under the guidance of my brother, Wayne, the house had been completely restored from its being devastated just two years earlier by the flood waters in the aftermath of Hurricane Katrina. As I stood in the newly renovated den, I realized that there were still places in New Orleans yet to be restored, and I came face to face with unattended grief still residing in me about what had happened to my beloved place of birth, and why. In the stillness, I heard healing words that have never left me:

Rest Leads to Peace.
Peace Leads to Clarity.
Clarity Leads to Creativity.

I understood more deeply than ever before that there was a power on the backside of rest, strong enough to recover from any and every storm, either from without or from within.

BLESS WHAT YOU'VE GOT

During the writing of this book, I was privileged to hear my beloved friend, Dr. Robert A.F. Turner, Senior Pastor of the magnificent St. John Baptist Church in Columbia, Maryland, deliver a soul-stirring sermon at our church, entitled "There's No Limit to What God Can Do." The sermon was based on the famous biblical story in which

Jesus feeds the multitude with a child's lunch of five loaves of bread and two fish.

One of the highlights of a sermon rich with them was Dr. Turner observing that an unsung part of the miracle was Jesus choosing to bless what had been given him. Jesus gave thanks for the little he held in his hand, before making something so amazing happen, that we are still marveling over it 2000 years later.

Instead of bemoaning what you don't have, start blessing what you've got.

Jesus practiced the same pre-miracle blessing strategy on the day he raised Lazarus as he had on the day he raised a lavish meal from little. Is it just a coincidence that gratitude is the drum major leading the way for impossible possibilities in both instances? Or, can it be that where causing new life is concerned, gratitude is the best drum major of all.

NURTURING A GRATITUDE MIND-SET

The Rev. Frederick Streets tells the story of being warmly hosted at a home in a small village.

As he spoke with the adults, he noticed a little girl, and slipped his hand in his pocket to give her a few pieces of gum. After he finished speaking with his adult hosts, he was escorted outside, where he saw the little girl again. This time, she was seated in a circle surrounded by other children. Tears came to Dr. Streets' eyes when he realized what she was doing. She was sharing the pieces of gum he had just given her moments ago with her friends. From a moment of mere kindness, came a moment of majestic communion between a little girl and her friends.

Gratitude is effectively cultivated through an abiding sense of our having all we need, and enough to share with others.

CHAPTER 2

An Inspired Attitude Enhances Perception

§

"If you change the way you look at things,
the things you look at change."

--Dr. Wayne Dyer

Attitude Makes a Difference

The late Jacqueline Mary du Pre' was an English cellist. Because of multiple sclerosis, she was forced to stop performing at the age of 28. But by then, she was regarded as one of the most gifted cellists the world had ever known. Jacqueline du Pre' entered her first competition as a cellist when she was just six years old. On that day, she ran down the hall, carrying her cello above her head, with a big grin on her face. Someone standing by interpreted the child's demeanor as that of one who was elated with the relief of a successfully completed performance. He said to her, "I see you've just had your chance to play!" Young Jackie responded, "No, no I'm just about to!" Her enflamed attitude, which characterized her short but legendary performing life, was present from the beginning.

Attitude makes a difference.

Disposition makes a difference.

Mental Posture makes a difference.

A deathly attitude is unable to call forth new life; it takes a lively attitude to call forth new life.

A LIVELY ATTITUDE AND NEW LIFE
By lively attitude, I mean a disposition characterized by enthusiasm and possibility. It need not be completely bereft of concern and even fear, but such states have their say without taking the day. Having and holding a lively attitude is challenging, because people around us may have deathly attitudes. Deathly attitudes, dispositions riddled with negativism, bitterness, and resentment, are contagious.

If we are not careful we can very easily catch someone else's deathly attitude. This can be as mild as becoming less joyful simply because a weather reporter calls a rainy day a dreary day, and as substantial as becoming angry with someone because someone else has become angry with them.

Defending oneself against deadly attitudes aimed at us and or surrounding us is an important ability to cultivate.

Jesus might have caught the deathly attitude of Mary and Martha that day:

"If you had been here, our brother would not have died."

No, they didn't come right out and say it, but they implied that it was Jesus' fault that Lazarus was no longer with them. Had Jesus bought into that thinking and compounded it with his own self-diminishing guilt and shame, he may never have made it to the tomb.

Not only did Jesus have to protect himself from the accusation of two sisters who were hurting, but against the assessment of a crowd of people who determined that with a friend like Jesus, who couldn't be counted on in a time of desperate need, who needed enemies? Had Jesus bought into such condemning perceptions, he may have never made it to the tomb.

And it's not just the hurtful things that people say that can harm our attitude, but our repeating in our minds what they've said. Jesus might have, in the language of Parker Palmer, "conspired with his own diminishment" by choosing to replay the negative things people said about him.

Be careful of what you choose to replay in your mind. What we focus on expands.

We rise or fall on the tapes we choose to replay in our minds. Our attitudes are determined by what we choose to tell ourselves over and over again, by what we choose to keep repeating to ourselves.

Iconic composers and musicians Ray Charles and Quincy Jones, used to share a saying with each other, as a defense against the death-liness of racism and segregation "not one drop," their coded short-ened version of *"Not one drop of my self-worth depends on another's acceptance of me."*

Without tapes of worthiness to encourage and build us up, tapes of diminishment can destroy us, killing us softly without our ever being aware of it.

Jesus' Lively Attitude Tape
Speaking of tapes, here is one that always helps to cultivate a lively attitude: one entitled "God is with Me." We can hear this tape in Jesus' prayer:

"I thank you that you heard me, and I know that You always hear me."

In order to maintain a lively attitude, remember the times you knew God was with you, and God had heard you.

Jesus kept his attitude alive by recounting instances of God being alive in him and with him...

In the wilderness

At the wedding feast.

In the Storm.

And More.

Remembering that and how God is with us is a potent way of maintaining a lively attitude.

Being Freshly Enthused

In her marvelous book, *The Fire Starter Sessions*, author Danielle Laporte, shares an experience with her son who was then just 4 year old. She writes:

> *We went to a local ice cream parlor for a treat. It was a soft summer evening, just perfectly perfect, and we sat in the parlor's garden, under twinkly lights, licking our cones, not saying much. "So," I said through chocolate licks, "What's it feel like to be alive, like how's your life?" And without missing a beat, and with a slight cowboy lilt, he replied, "Oh Mama! It's ahhh-MAZing. If I were a telephone, I'd be ringin' all the time!"*

Perhaps Jesus said, "Except you become as a child, you can't enter into the kingdom," because he wanted us to make the connection between spirituality and being enthused, excited, and delighted with life.

God does not intend for children to have a monopoly on enthusiasm.

Enthusiasm derives from "en theos," "In God." To be enthused is to be in God. *There is not that much difference between someone who has stopped breathing, and someone who has lost their enthusiasm for life.* An Early Church Father, Irenaeus, said, "The Glory of God is a person fully alive."

Lightening Our Attitude with Grace

A Strange Daydream

I once daydreamed about God having a problem. God's problem was not the devil or sin. I imagined God having effectively addressed both those problems at Calvary. In my daydream, believe it or not, God's problem was religion. The problem was layered. First, religion placed God far away. Second, religion often portrayed God as being accessible only to the truly holy. Finally, religion presented belief and faith in ways that felt heavy and burdensome.

As I continued to let myself be taken away by these sudden and strangely compelling observations, I began to sense that of the three shortcomings, religion's tendency to present the spiritual quest as burdensome seemed to bother God the most. When I asked why this was so, a reply fell immediately and clearly upon my spirit:

Because even if you understand that I am close and available to all, if your experience with Me feels burdensome, I may as well be far off and attainable to only a few.

How heavy is your faith experience? Does it tend to weigh you down or lift you up?

The wonderful writer, Frederick Buechner, suggests that the certain sign that someone is in communion with God is that they evidence a "strange lightness of heart." Nothing lightens the heart better than God's grace, that divine blessing of supreme affirmation which inspires us to live *from* acceptance and not *for* acceptance. How might we rest and revel in such glad acceptance daily?

MAKE SPACE FOR WONDERING

Though my calling as a boy preacher was a source of great pride to my parents, they were sometimes concerned about my studying too much. My mother, in particular, offered a sternly worded warning that I never fully understood until many years later. She would say, "Let your mind rest, before your head busts open like a morning glory." The image makes me smile now. Her point was that, whatever my genuine religious calling was, I would do it and myself untold damage by not withdrawing myself from it for a while. Now, not only have I developed a genuine appreciation for mental rest, but for the rich dimensions of spirituality that may only be traversed through the complete thoughtlessness of a rested state.

Let your thinking at times yield to wondering: soft open-reflecting and non-reflecting, that you may be blown away by insight not accessible through rationale striving.

David puts it this way in Psalm 46:10

"Be still, and know that I am God."

The extraordinary poet, Mary Oliver, experiences this holy ground as a space of "not-thinking, not-remembering, and not-wanting." In addition to the peaceful enchantment offered by the cessation of mental engagement, there is something else about stillness and the emptiness that it allows for, which makes it particularly compelling given the sub-topic of lightening our attitude with grace: *Wondering is weightless.*

WATCH HOW YOU CARRY HEAVY LOADS

I worked my way through college as a stock clerk. My training involved learning how to lift and carry heavy loads. For example, to lift safely and easier I learned how to use my leg muscles and not my back muscles. Also, I learned to kneel and squat to pick something up, as opposed to bending over, and the importance of keeping my back, shoulders, and neck as straight as possible. When it came to carrying a heavy load, I learned to carry objects close to my body, and when possible, to carry objects directly in front of me rather than on the sides of my body. That way, the muscles on one or the other side did not have to do all the work. In short, I learned, in the words of one of my supervisors, "how to work the work, as opposed to letting the work, work me."

Often, it wasn't the weight of the load that made it feel so heavy, but the way I chose to carry it. Similarly, in life, it's not just the weight of the load that makes it feel so heavy, but the way we choose to carry it. A better way to carry a heavy load in life is to focus less on the burden and more on God, Our Gracious Burden-Bearer.

No matter how deep our pain, God's love is deeper.

TAKE A DIP IN GOD'S GRACE EACH DAY

Once while vacationing on beautiful Lake George in upstate New York, I noticed persons out swimming at the break of day. I later found out that they were participating in the daily scheduled "Morning Dip." That morning dip prompted me to start one of my own: taking moments each day, sometimes several times a day, imagining myself wading, swimming, and floating in the soothing waters of God's grace. These are moments of unspeakable ease when I not only remember God's love, but I let myself feel God's love afresh in the moment.

There is nothing more blessed then a tender heart. Take care of yours by soaking it in God's grace each day.

GRACE SPARKS ARE EVERYWHERE

Once while waiting for a plane, a young girl began playing peek-a-boo with me while seated on her mother's lap. Whenever, I looked in her direction, she would playfully hide her eyes, until one time when she didn't. In that moment, I caught sight of pure love in her wondrous gaze. There God was again. Sometimes we miss the grace we think we ought to have because we are standing right smack dab in the middle of it.

A doable and effective way to receive grace anew each day is to notice little messages that God sends each day directly to us, through others, via our labor and leisure, and by way of nature.

Anything that opens the mind or softens the heart has God's fingerprints all over it.

I call such messages and experiences "Grace Sparks," and I am collecting them all the time. I'll say more about them later.

I have never forgotten my daydream about God's problem. But it has been delightfully overshadowed by daily grace practices that make the load of living lighter. I am encouraged to keep on keeping on in this way by the Graced Son who says with a smile, "My yoke is easy and my burden is light."

The Power of Self-Perception

Despite what was said to him and about him, Jesus still felt confident enough to preside at a public resurrection.

Jesus' self-perception as the beloved and empowered Son of God was still firmly in place. Given what was said to him by distraught sisters and critical observers, he may have left town without ever visiting the tomb. He may have allowed his spirit to be crushed to the point of being unwilling and unable to manifest the power of resurrection welling up inside of him. And that's just it, no matter what the naysayers said, what was in Jesus was greater than what was against Jesus

What's in you is greater than what's against you!

The question is, "Can you own what's in you?"

Can you own your inner glory?

An empowered self-perception strong enough to withstand the diminishing assessments of others is crucial to our calling forth new life. There can be no accessing power that we allow to be talked down in us, or spoken completely out of us.

Affirming our sacred esteem and strength is something we may do daily. Pay attention to the inspirations that come your way which remind you of your inner glory. The poem, *My Brilliant Image*, by the legendary Persian poet, Hafiz, and translated by Daniel Ladinsky, is a fixture on my desk at home. In it, the sun reveals the source of its majestic shine to be the "Infinite Incandescence" of humanity. The sun praises "The Astonishing Light" of our own being. You may read the brief poem in its entirety in *I Heard God Laughing: Poems of Hope and Joy*. How can you afford to pass on a book with such a title?

Reading inspired words often inspires some of my own:

Guess What!

We look upon angels

and say,

"WOW!"

Guess what!

Angels look upon us

and say

the same thing!

You Too

What if

at the conclusion of your singing,

"How Great Thou Art,"

you heard God whisper,

"You too"?

Why not?

Your glory is,

after all,

God's idea.

YOUR OWN CLOTHES ARE GOOD ENOUGH

I find it astonishing to believe that I am on the back side of a 25-year seminary teaching career at Andover Newton Theological School. It seems like only yesterday that I was fearfully contemplating leaving the full-time pastorate for full-time teaching. I feared that though I may have had what it took to teach a course here and there, I did not have all it took to contribute to the academy in a fine and full way. More specifically, I wondered if my passions for preaching and pastoring would enhance my role as a professor or diminish it.

When the teaching opportunity presented itself, I hesitated. In the middle of my hesitation, I had a dream one night. In the dream, I was standing outside a school building, reluctant to join an academic processional that was underway. In an instant, I was questioned by an unseen presence about my holding back and not processing with the others. I responded, "I am not dressed appropriately." I will never forget the ready and firm reply that unleashed me toward a teaching ministry that has been wonder on wonder: "Go in wearing your own clothes."

Trust who you are and what you have been given. Allow such trust to buttress your confidence and sanctified self-perception.

With an ever-enhanced perception of ourselves, we can stride freely and fully on the terrain of calling forth new life for ourselves, and in various ways, in our relationships and organizational living. Without it, we shrink in the face of magnificent continual empowerment that we can never give ourselves permission to believe or accept. Believing and accepting such is exactly what God has in mind. Indeed, the great holy presumption of Pentecost, the infusion of the early church with the Holy Spirit, is that we will not find empowered living to be too overwhelming.

No matter what, believe in yourself and have faith in your unique offering to the world—and don't hold back.

CHAPTER 3
An Enhanced Perception
Unleashes New Possibilities

§

"To live in the Spirit is to hear the
rhythms of new possibilities
and not be afraid to play along."

JESUS *IN VISIONS* NEW LIFE

THE ONLY THING MATCHING THE horrible fact that Lazarus was already dead, was the hallelujah counter-fact that Lazarus was already risen in Jesus' mind. Jesus saw Lazarus raised from the dead before he actually raised him from the dead. The hints are in what Jesus said even before making the journey to Judea, as recorded in chapter 11 of John's gospel:

"This sickness is not unto death, but for the glory of God, that the Son of God may be glorified through it." (11:4)

"Our friend sleeps, but I go that I may wake him up." (11:11)

"I am glad for your sakes that I was not there that you may believe." (11:15)

Upon his arrival, Jesus found himself up against a grief that was as thick as a wall. What broke through the wall was his confident compassion:

"I am the resurrection and the life. He who believes in Me, though he may die, he shall live. And whoever lives and be-lieves in Me shall never die...." (11:25-26)

In Jesus' mind, Lazarus was already raised before he got there. Before he arrived at the tomb, Jesus viewed resurrection with his imagination, or *saw* resurrection in his spirit. He felt resurrection deep down within, or *sensed* resurrection in his heart. He had full peace concerning what was to occur, or *settled* on resurrection in his soul.

Jesus *In-Visioned* new life. *In-Visioning* is imagining with our to-tal being. It is using our God-given gifts of mind, body, and soul to participate in the godly action of creating and manifesting desires and dreams.

The day Lazarus was raised, *In-Visioning* unleashed a creative energy so divine in nature that God could not help but respond--*Sacred Energy Attracted Sacred Energy.*

Sacred Energy Still Attracts Sacred Energy!

I am blessed to serve as pastor of the magnificent Zion Baptist Church in Lynn, Massachusetts. One of the things that created an instant bond between us was the way so many congregants express their love, their divine lavish appreciation for each other and visitors with ready and effortless displays of affection, including hearty laughter, vigorous handshakes, and some of the warmest hugs you will find anywhere on earth. I shared my sentiments with a nun at an ecumenical Good Friday service soon after my arrival. She smiled, and proceeded to tell me that she fully understood, and why. She spoke of having driven past the church once. Because she had known its witness of compassionate and dedicated work in the community, she blew a kiss toward the building. What she said next sent chills of confirmation through my being. She said, "Pastor Kirk, after I blew that kiss, something happened to me that I will remember for the rest of my life. Suddenly I felt an energy wave of love rushing back toward me. It was as if the Zion Baptist Church sanctuary was blowing a kiss back at me."

Sacred Energy Still Attracts Sacred Energy!

Using Your Sacred Energy to *In-Vision* New Life

In-Visioning is divine dynamic creative power attracting dynamic creative power. Such layered energy holds resurrection power, with the strength to bring forth what is already manifested within, into fresh, fine, and full formation, without. The world that we create within us is the world that flourishes around us. Lazarus more readily comes forth around you, if he has already come forth, in your spirit, heart, and soul, within you.

You may practice the same *In-Visioning* Jesus did in order to call forth new life today, if you dare to *see* new life in your spirit, *sense* new life in your heart, and *settle* new life in your soul. Giving *sight, feeling,* and *peace* to your dreams cultivates sustained spiritual energy to call them to full manifestation in the world.

For more detailed guidance on practicing *In-Visioning*, please see *The In-Visioning Journal*, the companion guide created to help you generate fresh clarity, focus, and energy to achieve your desires and goals, whenever you wish and as often as you choose to. By regularly engaging a 3-step process of seeing in your spirit, sensing in your heart, and settling in your spirit, you will unlock potent unused inner powers necessary for unusual achievement. How much unused spiritual energy do you have? Find out.

Here are a few suggestions for *In-Visioning* based on my experience with this dynamic and doable practice:

* **Explore Early Morning Sessions.** The early-morning mind is ripe for fresh considerations and imaginings. I write in my book, *Fulfilled: Living and Leading with Unusual Wisdom, Peace, and Joy*: "*As we awaken with fresh energy and renewed enthusiasm, early day provides a spacious playground for creative and meaningful inspiration and reflection....The early-morning mind*

has the luxury of not having been barnstormed by the demands, pressures, and worries of the day. Such early morning spaciousness should not be wasted."

● **Be Lighthearted.** Though the matters you consider may be serious in nature, to be lighthearted about them is to be more open and welcoming of all possibilities.

Rigidity is stifling. Your playful heart never ceases to be one of your most potent strengths. Prolific thinker and blogger Seth Godin's reflection about business leaders and innovation can be applied to all of us and creation: *It's impossible to do innovation in any field with your arms crossed and a scowl on your face.* Have fun framing and forging your future with God.

● **Repeat Sessions.** Repetition is a proven effective teaching and learning strategy. Use repetition in your *In-Visioning* practice, by using some sessions to re-do prior sessions. This is especially effective for manifesting significant achievements that require extended time. For example, I repeated numerous sessions in which I imaged this book coming forth as an empowering flame, and being spread by persons who would be inspired to catch and spread the fire. It is important when repeating sessions to experience the new session in fresh ways, and be open to inspired alterations from the initial experience.

● **Celebrate New Life Come Forth.** Noting that and when new life comes forth will encourage you to keep taking responsibility for calling forth new life. You will do so because you know how, because you can, and because it works. There is no greater feeling than to be walking in the territory of your sanctified strength. Do not be afraid of your holy power.

The fabulous holy presumption of Pentecost is that we will not find divine empowerment to be too overwhelming.

- **Remember Gratitude, Attitude, and Perception.** *Gratitude inspires attitude. An inspired attitude enhances perception. An enhanced perception unleashes new possibilities.* As you engage each session, be thankful, positive, and open. Such chosen postures make us supple for the Spirit's moving in our lives in adventurous and wondrous ways. *Leave your mind's window wide open for the fresh wind of divine possibility.*

- **Be Peaceful in Your Practice.** Anxiety and stress dilute and diminish our creative capacities. Practice *In-Visioning* with a calm spirit. To facilitate such peace, I find it helpful to play meditative music at a low volume. Also, candle light can help to promote an attitude of peace.

  Inner peace is an unsung superpower. From a calm spirit comes forth the strength to move mountains—and call forth new life!

- **Be Open to Surprise Inspiration.** One of the exciting and enchanting parts of *In-Visioning* for me is seeing and sensing things I had not planned on. When we open our spirits to God's Spirit, we can't help but receive impressions and imaginings that expand our world. Be open to new aspirations, desires, and possibilities.

Poet, Ranier Rilke, writes, *"Most people come to know only one corner of their room, on one narrow strip on which they keep walking back and forth."*

Evidence your openness by keeping a notepad or recording device nearby as you *In-Vision*. This places you in a posture of expectancy and readiness to capture impressions, mental images, and phrases for future reference and contemplation. Be open to the ways God will begin to expand your horizon, and impact your dreams and expectations for the wildly wonderful best. Be open to unusual inspiration. We may have problems with the unexpected and unfamiliar, but God doesn't. God's favorite language is "surprise."

To live in the Spirit is to hear the rhythms of new possibilities and not be afraid to play along.

In-Visioning is not just another chore for me, *In-Visioning* is playing with fire. Part of our endowment as the children of God is the power to create. By divine decree, God has called us to be co-creators with God. In order to live God's dream of dynamic creative partnership, we are challenged to become more aware of and more adept at utilizing our creative powers of imagination. *In-Visioning* is a method for you to hone your power to create, which though being very sacred, has to do with the very human skills of *clarifying* and *focusing*.

In-Visioning is a way of regularly and purposefully harnessing and maximizing our creative spiritual ability to call forth new life.

Jesus didn't seem to have a problem with exploring and practicing his unique sacred strength. What about you?

THE POWER LINE OF CLARITY

I have worn contact lenses since high school. From hard lenses I used to take out and clean each evening, to soft lenses I simply toss into the trash at night, I have always been amazed by how such a tiny thing can make such a huge difference. Without my lenses, just a few feet ahead of me is a blurry mass. With the lenses, clarity reigns supreme, giving me the ability to focus on one thing as opposed to another, and the confidence to move intentionally and deliberately in the direction of my focus. Though perhaps not discernible at first glance, clarity carries enormous power.

Let's follow the power line of clarity for a moment. When it comes to meeting any objective, clarity is the critical first key. Through clarity, we identify just what it is we want to accomplish. With the objective clearly in mind, we are free to direct all of our energies toward it and not anything else. Thus, clarity facilitates fine and full focus on a singular objective. The finer and fuller focusing of energies fuels optimal engagement and performance. Optimal engagement leads to achievement.

> *Clarity leads to fine and full focus.*
> *Fine and full focus leads to optimal engagement.*
> *Optimal engagement leads to achievement.*

Clarity is the unsung fantastic first factor in the resurrection of Lazarus. From the beginning, Jesus was crystal clear about the status of the situation, beyond what appeared visible on the surface. He sensed that God was up to something, took his time, and remained clear on the prospect of resurrection even as the sentiments of fearful disciples, distraught sisters, and unenlightened observers sought to blur his vision. Jesus never allowed his vision to be blurred. Jesus was able to raise Lazarus, in part, because in his own mind, he was clear about doing so. His clarity fed a fine and full focus on new life. Supported by such clarity and focus, Jesus was able to harness and direct his spiritual energy toward optimal engagement with death in the graveyard, resulting in the biggest headline in town for a long, long time.

The headline, "Lazarus is Alive," is made possible by the power of God manifested through the power line of clarity.

Said the Angel with the Biggest Smile

"Be radically receptive
to completely fresh imaginings,
undiluted by self-imposed limitations,
and filled to running over with unadulterated possibility.
I dare you!"
Said the angel with the biggest smile.

Keep Getting Got By God!

God is a Divine Prankster,

Who loves playing holy jokes on people,

and shouting,

"Got you!"

What else is there to do but

keep getting got by God!

CHAPTER 4

Falling in Love with Your Transformation

§

"Take a chance; play things you've never heard."

--Betty Carter, Jazz Singer

Lazarus Struggles

In his novel, *Lazarus*, Alain Absire imagines Lazarus coming back to life in these words:

> *He was being shaken. Why? He could hear voices shouting, close but indistinct. Still, he couldn't breathe. At last he felt the bag being lifted from his face, and he tried to inhale. But his chest, heavy as stone, scarcely moves, and the little air he got was scorching hot. He tried to look around, to turn his head despite the stiffness in his neck. But there was a white veil before his eyes, and all he could see were patches of light, and moving shadows beyond. People were touching his mouth, his forehead,...He was gripped from all sides, squeezed. He wanted to shout to them to let go, but could utter only a long groan.*

They were untying him now, and suddenly his hands were free. But when he lifted his arm, it was as heavy as lead, and he had to let it fall again.

The last line is a sign of things to come for the Lazarus of Absire's novel.

But when he lifted his arm, it was as heavy as lead, and he had to let it fall again.

The rest of Absire's novel is about a Lazarus who never gets beyond the heaviness of his new life. For him, resurrection is more burden than liberation. The great tragedy is that Absire's Lazarus never finds joy in living a resurrected life. Resurrection is more imposition than inspiration, more oppression than opportunity.

Fall in Love with Your Transformation

I am writing this on the day after celebrating our 35th Engagement Anniversary. That's right, we not only celebrate our Wedding, but our engagement. One of the reasons is that my wife and I became engaged after just 12 days of dating. I would have asked her sooner, but I didn't want to alarm her. That it was during the fall in New England, a time of beautiful transformation in nature, enhanced the enchantment of it all even more. Being able to link transformation to enchantment has surrounded change with allurement for me. I see change, less as a struggle, and more as an astonishing adventure, worthy of far more delight than dread.

Rather than being something to fear, change can be something we choose to fall in love with.

When it comes to accepting and celebrating change, how we perceive change influences how and if we experience change.

Though change is challenging, it is important to understand that we are not limited to viewing change exclusively in terms of stress, strain, and struggle. In fact, perceiving it that way helps to construct that reality. Change need not, first or only, be perceived as something negative, uncomfortable, and grueling. We need not always struggle through change. Sometimes we may even dance transformation.

LETTING GO
To let ourselves fall in love with what is to be, we must be able to let go of what used to be.

You can't let go and hold on at the same time.

Part of the problem with Absire's Lazarus is that he would rather be who he used to be.

In the novel, he keeps looking and feeling for who he once was. Lazarus resisted new life by constantly reaching back for his old life!

We can't truly live in the present while trying to live in the past at the same time.

What are you trying to hold on to?

What are you refusing to let go of?

No matter how glorious the past, choosing to live there is choosing to live in a tomb.

Life is about going on, and to go on well we must constantly release something we've held to grasp something we are being invited to hold on to. In her classic book by the same title, Judith Viorst calls such relinquishing, "necessary losses." She declares that "losing is the price we pay for living."

The poet, Lucille Clifton, envisions a more tranquil, if not beautiful, releasing in her majestic, *blessing the boats*, which encourages as follows:

> *kiss the wind then turn from it....*
> *and may you in your innocence*
> *sail through this to that.*

Howard Thurman's prayer may be your prayer as well:

> *Keep alive in me the forward look, the high hope,*
>
> *The onward surge. Let me not be frozen*
>
> *Either by the past or the present.*

<u>LIVING ONWARD AND UPWARD</u>
Fear, the great enemy of change, meets its match in curiosity. Curiosity is the first and continuing step of living onward and upward in a life of continual transformation.

Curiosity is the unsung remedy for fear.

Begin to muster interest in something you are afraid of, and watch wonder take the place of worry. Being curious is a way of falling in love with transformation. What are we to be curious about? New explorations and discoveries. New challenges and learnings.

New ways of experiencing life and the world. Such enlivening curiosity is the spirit in the following declaration about singing a particular musical selection by Jazz singer, Betty Carter:

> *I am educating myself as I go along and learning more about myself, and then putting my voice to the test on top of that, challenging it, making sure that it stays on top and does not drop. So I'm challenging the whole picture and taking what I call a risk.*

The wild wonderful truth is that the spirit of discovery Carter manifests in regard to journeying through a musical selection in fresh new ways, may be applied to all of life. And, grace on grace, there is no charge to be new each day: **N**otice, **E**xplore, **W**onder.

New life is no afterthought in the mind of God; it is at the heart of God's will. This is the spirit behind Isaiah heralding:

> *But they that wait upon the Lord shall renew their strength; they shall mount up with wings as eagles; they shall run, and not be weary; and they shall walk and not faint.*

Encouraging us to fully embrace God's new life agenda in the here and now, John O'Donohue concludes his magnificent poem, *For a New Beginning*:

Awaken your spirit to adventure;

Hold nothing back, learn to find ease in risk;

Soon you will be home in a new rhythm,

For your soul senses the world that awaits you.

DEVELOPING A LEVELING UP MINDSET

Video gaming is one of my favorite hobbies. In addition to providing hours of fun, games provided fruitful bonding time with each of our four children. To this day, I still enjoy sports games with our son who now has 3 children of his own. In addition to the fun and the family sharing, believe it or not, video games have proven to be a formidable teacher. One of the greatest lessons it's taught me is the importance of strategizing for and anticipating "leveling up."

Leveling up is the gaming term for achieving sufficient amounts of experience and victories to proceed to higher grades of performance and challenge. Leveling up is especially important in role playing games, such as the astonishing Skyrim, in which your character begins with limited means, and then through your strategic engaging play, becomes a mighty force of nature fearless in adventure and fierce in challenging encounters. The fun is not just in discovery and conquest, but in creatively managing your character's growth and development, and in anticipating and manifesting your new empowerment.

Why should such potent energy be limited to the realm of video gaming? Seeing ourselves new can be an integral part in bringing forth new life, in real life. When was the last time you seriously reflected on your own development or leveling up as a person? In what specific areas of your life do you wish to see improvement? Are you basically leaving your leveling up to chance? How might you become better at deliberately planning leveling up? Leveling up is not just a goal for a video game; it is a goal for life. We may be new persons continually. Just imagine how much anticipation and excitement you could create for your life if you believed in and practiced continual leveling up as a way of life.

The benefits of leveling up as a way of life are enormous. You can expect and wield new strength each day in varying aspects and dimensions of your life. Your only limitation would be your own restricted imagination. The possibilities for your growth and new life possibilities are endless. And chances are, the learning and leveling up doesn't stop here. What if eternity is a continuation of the holy leveling up that we begin in life? Deeply owning a sense of your capacity for endless expansion can release an inner exuberance unlike anything you have ever experienced.

One of the benefits of a leveling up mindset is the transformed way you begin to face persistent challenges in your life. What if all of your challenges had to face a new more formidable you each day? Think of one thing in particular that is chronically difficult to handle. You may be unknowingly contributing to your stifling entrenchment with your stagnate personal assessment, attitude, and expectation. What if you begin to see yourself stronger each time you come upon the challenge?

That persistent challenge has faced All you had then; it has never faced All you have now.

Your *All* is always being enhanced, especially if you are intentional and consistent about ensuring that it is. Get into the habit of affirming your intentional growth by embracing your fresh strength, each new day. Such a practice is a wonderfully doable way of calling forth new life.

P.S. For provocative insights on the social appeal and creative power of video gaming, see two books by Jane McGonigal: *Reality is Broken* and *Super Better*.

THE STRENGTH OF SINGULAR FOCUS

Part of falling in love with your transformation is falling in love with the *process and practices* associated with calling forth new life. This means becoming more curious about and better capable of maximizing powers that most of us never come close to using at optimal levels. One such ability is the power of focusing.

I am willing to bet that all the significant accomplishments of your life, especially the most challenging ones have at least one thing in common: focus. You consciously and unconsciously directed your spiritual, mental, and physical energy toward what you desired. When your focus wavered, you re-focused. You kept directing and re-directing your energy toward what you desire. I am also willing to bet that the greater the challenge, the more you focused on that challenge exclusively. You did not allow your attention to be diverted for long, if at all, from that which you were most focused on. What you were using, either on purpose or unintentionally, was the power of singular and sustained focus.

Concentrated focus, or singular and sustained focus, is the common denominator of all achievement. What we think about the most and most often and intently is what we are most likely to do in life. Think of the things that you have accomplished in life. There was a direct correlation between that accomplishment and your heartfelt thoughts, your energized focus. You got an idea; you started thinking about it more and more; your thoughts inspired action. Thus, you accomplished in your life what was originally a thought in your mind.

The bridge between thought and deed is focus.

There is an essential integration between what we imagine, what we focus our minds on, and final action. See imagination, focus, and action as three integrated realities.

The benefits of focus are enormous. Focus does the following and more:

* Melts procrastination.
* Generates new ideas.
* Attracts people and situations helpful to your purpose.
* Provides mental, physical, emotional, and spiritual energy to fuel action.
* Inspires a persevering spirit, allowing you to overcome discouragement.

As stated in Chapter 3, Jesus used the power of focus in order to raise Lazarus. Moreover, his focus was not diverted or diminished by multiple objectives. Multi-tasking is highly overrated. Not only do we observe the power of focus in Jesus, but the power of singular focus.

There is unusual concentrated strength in a singular focus.

> *When Jesus raised Lazarus from the dead,*
> *he wasn't trying to do anything else at the same time.*

We diminish our creative dynamism by trying to do too much at the same time. While we may be able to accomplish some trivial tasks, mindlessly and simultaneously, formidable challenges require undiluted and sustained focus. As you become more committed to a lifestyle of calling forth new life over and over again, you will understand and be convinced of the need to prioritize and focus on just a few things at any given time.

How much new life can you call forth using the power of a singular focus, deliberately and on purpose? There is only one way to find out.

The Morning ARC: Grab Hold of Your Focus First Thing

The Morning ARC is a simple 3-step habit I developed to take control of my mind during the first moments of being awake. I find if I don't take charge first thing, my mind can ramble in ways that aren't very creative or productive. If I don't take control of my thoughts as soon as I become conscious, sometimes it is easy for me to be carried away by mental negativity that drags my spirit down before the day begins. Sometimes we do ourselves in with the way we think before we get out of the bed in the morning. I've found the Morning ARC to be an effective method for setting my mind for optimal effectiveness and positivity upon arising from sleep. It is a simple doable method for establishing control over your focus at the beginning of your day.

What does ARC mean? A stands for **Awareness**. R stands for **Relinquish**. C stands for **Create**. Begin your Morning ARC with establishing mental awareness. Once you are up, begin to ask yourself questions like:

What's on my mind?
What did I dream last night?
How do I feel?

The goal is to just become aware of your mental state. By simply becoming more aware of what's on your mind, you flip the control switch to "on." Your thoughts don't control you; you control them. How do you know this? You have the ability to observe them, to be aware of what you are thinking.

Secondly, lose or *relinquish* thoughts that you have determined through past experience aren't healthy for you, including harsh thoughts about yourself, others, and life in general. *Picture yourself waving such thoughts on and out of your mental skies.* Be careful not to relinquish unpleasing thoughts too quickly. Sometimes the thoughts that trouble us have something to teach us. It is wise to interrogate a thought that troubles us before dismissing it as having no value.

Finally, begin to *create* or think thoughts that inspire and enliven you! Since you have to think about something, instead of thinking depressing thoughts that bring you down, intentionally focus on thoughts that lift you up. Since what we focus on expands, why not insure that what's expanding within us is enhancing and not diminishing us?

The *Morning ARC* has become second nature to me now. Give it a try. Hopefully, it will have the same positive impact on you as it has had on me. If *ARC* doesn't work for you, think of another way to activate your focus power first thing in the morning. There is simply too much creative power in our mental focusing not to be increasingly deliberate and skillful at using it. Calling forth new life is enhanced immeasurably by optimal focusing. Moreover, an enhanced ability to focus is part of what it means to live anew each day. Every dimension of who we are is potentially refreshed each day, including, if not especially, our minds.

OPEN TO NEW KNOWING

Martha is the unsung heroine of John 11. Throughout the story, she evidences a childlike, compelling capacity for *open knowing*: knowing always ending with a comma, never a period. For example, though Jesus' tardiness may have been a factor in Lazarus' death, Martha knows according to verse 22, that even now God will give whatever Jesus asks. And her *open knowing* is visible again. Though she knows that resurrection is reserved for the last day, she is open to Jesus' startling and striking *new knowing* in verse 25: "I am the resurrection and the life. Those who believe in me, even though they die, will live, and everyone who lives and believes in me will never die. Do you believe this?"

Martha does not say, "That's preposterous" and walk off. She does not say, "I am sad, not insane." She does not think to herself, "Resurrection and life! He's good, but not that good." But rather, she lets his words in. They tingle inside. And she wades out into the cool, refreshing water of *new knowing*.

There is another biblical example of someone who remained in learning mode and open to new knowing. In chapter 3, verses 1-21 of John's Gospel, there is a record of a remarkable encounter between Jesus and a religious leader named Nicodemus. In this passage, we stand to learn as much from Nicodemus as we do from Jesus, although Jesus is doing most of the talking. Jesus is talking so much because Nicodemus keeps asking him questions: "How can anyone be born after having grown old?" "Can one enter a second time into the mother's womb and be born?" "How can these things be?" These are the questions we know about. Given the urgent matters being discussed and the intensity of the exchange, it is easy to believe that Nicodemus asked many more questions. This text is a picture of someone who, though accomplished, has opted to remain in learning mode, open to new knowing.

JOURNAL YOUR JOURNEY

I began journaling upon resigning my first full-time senior pastorate to pursue further graduate studies and a seminary teaching career. My main reason for writing almost every day in a small book filled with lined empty pages was that I didn't want to forget the wonderful persons I had loved, and the wondrous experiences we had shared, during an amazing time of ministry together at the newly founded Beacon Light Baptist Church in New Orleans, Louisiana. I felt compelled to reflect on what I had learned, and draw applications from such reflection to help me better determine where I was heading. Little did I know that I would keep journaling long past this major transition, and that my daily writing practice (which has gone through many different sized books of lined and unlined pages, and is now mainly being done via an iPad application called "Day One") would help me to prayerfully and intentionally navigate many more life adventures, in both my outer and inner worlds.

One of the greatest benefits of journaling for me is it being a consistently efficient and effective tool for genuine growth and transformation. Authentic change is not something to be passively desired, but something to be actively determined.

Enter journaling. Journaling is a way to take responsibility for and practice Deliberate, Creative, and Sustained personal transformation. By deliberate, I mean consciously and purposefully identifying specific areas in our lives where we wish to grow. By creative, I mean imagining and designing inspiring and practical strategies to cultivate our growth. By sustained, I mean mentally reviewing ways we have grown and are growing, and mentally previewing ways we wish to grow.

Life is a wondrous gift that none of us ever saw coming. Through the prayerful attention and intentional reflection of journaling, God's great gift becomes our great offering.

P.S. When journaling, note that questions are as important, if not more important, than answers. Here are three questions to get you started or urge you on in your "Journaling the Journey of Transformation Practice":

1. What specific ways am I seeking to grow as a child of God?
2. What am I presently curious about?
3. What rocks am I currently searching under?

CALLING FORTH INNER PEACE

One of the most frightening times of my life was experiencing burnout in my early 30s.

I had no idea what burnout or stress was. All I know is that while delivering a sermon, I came to a screeching halt. For weeks thereafter, I suffered with nervous anxiety. Even when I was cleared of any physical malady, fear about what I was going through and whether or not I would go through it again held me in emotional bondage.

During this time in the valley, I discovered a precious gem. And know this for sure, there are gems in the valley that cannot be found on the mountaintop. The gem I discovered was the power of a particular scripture to mediate instant peace. The scripture is Isaiah 26:3:

Thou wilt keep him in perfect peace, whose mind is stayed on thee: because he trusteth in thee.

When I arrived at a point of feeling almost overwhelmed by nervousness, I started repeating this scripture slowly and softly, sometimes silently and sometimes aloud. I discovered that doing so released peace into my being. It was as if I could feel peace seeping into me, and filling the place once held by fear. I noticed, as well, that it wasn't just the wondrous meaning of the words that was bringing solace to me, but the melodic sounds and rhythms of the words. The meaning and the music of the words brought healing to my mind. What a moment to realize that I could make peace by intentionally appropriating the meaning and music of Scripture.

When Jesus said, "Blessed are the peacemakers," perhaps he was speaking about us all, not just those laboring in the field of international diplomacy. We have the power to cultivate and make inner peace with our thoughts and words all the time. The challenge is to begin to become more aware of our peacemaking power, and more dedicated to mindfully using it in everyday life.

Peace is no passive thing. A peaceful spirit is most postured for splendid creation.

There are few things in life more dynamic than a soul at ease.

LIVE TO SOAR

While walking in my neighborhood one morning, I heard rustling in trees to my left. Suddenly, as I turned to look, a small red bird jetted across my path headed toward the other side of the street. A situation in which a collision is narrowly avoided is called a near miss. Perhaps this incident would qualify as such; when the bird crossed my path it could not have been more than fifteen yards away. On the other hand, this close encounter was anything but a near miss. You see, as the bird passed before me it dropped this question on me:

Do you think birds ever think, for a moment, that they shouldn't fly?

We miss out on so much adventure and assent because of hesitancy and fear. We cage ourselves in jail cells of low aspirations. We resist dreaming beyond our comfort zones. We end up accepting stale acceptableness as our living norm. We don't fly because we don't think we can or should.

CHAPTER 5

Down but Not Done

§

"I gotta' right to sing the blues."

--LOUIS ARMSTRONG

"There is a vitality, a life force, an energy, a quickening which is translated through you into action, and because there is only one of you in all time, this expression is unique. And, if you block it, it will never exist."

--MARTHA GRAHAM

"Down"

THE WORD "DOWN" IS OFTEN associated with something negative:

A house in disrepair is *run-down.*

An insult is a *put-down.*

A person who takes advantage of others and enjoys doing so is *low-down.*

A disappointment is a *let-down.*

The word and words similar are used a great deal to refer to our not feeling spirited: *down in the dumps, feeling down and out.*

We need to give *down* its due. We do ourselves and our faith a disservice when we act like we are always supposed to feel on top of the world. I am having stronger and stronger resistance to worship stylings that leave no room for those who don't feel emotionally high, or feel like shouting God's praise. Indeed, forcing persons into a praiseful posture may be a form of liturgical violence.

God did not try to make Jesus stop crying before the resurrection of Lazarus. Our tears matter.

Take Time to Tend to Your Wounds

As a pastor, I am privileged to be invited unto the lives of persons on the mountaintops and in the valleys of life, and everyplace in between. I laugh, cry, and wonder with persons younger and older. Pastoring is a tender calling. It is a calling in which persons invite you to view aspects and dimensions of their living that even beloved family members may not be allowed to see.

Knowing more about someone can be hurtful and helpful at the same time. This is never truer then when I hear of a conflict between persons, and make connections between the behaviors exhibited and the background information I have. A repeated reality is persons wounding others due to their own unattended wounds.

A particularly frequent manifestation of ripple effect wounding, or persons wounding others from the place of their hidden hurts, is someone rejecting others out of their own unhealed experiences of being rejected. Indeed, I consider un-considered and un-mended wounds of rejection to be one of the biggest hindrances to vibrant living that there is. Rejection hits us at our core, because we have a sacred instinctive desire to be accepted. When acceptance is withheld, it is as if the rug of life has been pulled out from under us.

The ultimate healing for rejection is God's grace. When we believe ourselves to be unconditionally beloved by God, we are free to live *from* acceptance and not *for* acceptance.

Grace frees us from the iron-grip of rejection. As we accept our divine acceptance, we are free to flow with unconditional love.

One of the most helpful things we can do for others is to tend to our wounds through a variety of means, including professional counseling, depth dialogues with trusted friends, journaling, and, of course, prayer. Tending to our wounds helps to keep us from wounding others unknowingly—and knowingly. Take time to tend to your wounds. Don't let unattended wounds keep you from unusual healing, and the new life it brings.

To Be Down is Not to be Done

Derek Redmond, a runner in the 400 meters, had been forced to withdraw from the 1988 Olympic Games in Seoul because of an Achilles tendon injury. He underwent five surgeries over the next year. Four years later, he arrived at the 1992 Olympic Games in Barcelona to win a medal.

He quickly took the lead in the semifinal race, and was on his way to qualifying for the finals, when he heard a pop in his right hamstring. He pulled up in agonizing pain. He began hopping on one leg, and then slowed down, and fell to the track. Medical personnel ran toward him.

But medical personnel weren't the only persons running toward him. Jim Redmond, Derek's father, was in the stands and saw his son go down. He immediately made his way to the track, sidestepping some and bumping into others, all the while identifying himself to track officials trying to halt his progress.

By the time Jim Redmond arrived on the track, though the race was over, his son had started limping toward the finish line. Jim got to his son about 120 meters from the finish line, wrapped his arm around his waist, and with 65,000 fans cheering them on, they finished the race.

There is a Fiercely Free Spirit in the world, forever seeking to inspire anyone choosing with the strength they have left, not to give up.

Being Raised By Grace Over and Over Again

My dear champion of a father, Frederick Jesse Jones, had two interesting, and to be completely honest, down right irritating driving habits. First, he used to drive around parking lots looking for the just right parking space. He would pass up what seemed like dozens of empty parking spaces looking for the perfect space, usually where he could read and watch the four of us while my mother shopped. The larger the parking lot, the longer the exploration.

My mother would plead with him to find a space, "Sometime today, Freddie." "I'm coming up on one," he would say. Mom would respond, "Christmas is coming, too."

The other habit which bothered me even more was his way of driving right upon the rear of other cars before coming to a complete stop. It was as if he was seeing how close he could get to the other car without hitting it. My mother had a few words to say to him about this too, but I can't say them here.

My father left little margin, room, space between vehicles. Maybe we do something like that when it comes to grace. How much space do you allow for God's unmerited favor in your life?

New Life at the Pace of Grace
Let's consider another resurrection event for a moment: the resurrection of Jesus himself from the dead. How Jesus came back to life matters almost as much as the fact that he did.

When Jesus came back to life, he took his time to lovingly greet Mary, casually walk with two persons who thought he was a stranger on the Emmaus Road, gracefully address Thomas's doubts, and gently encourage and reassure Peter. There is excitement in his return, but no hurry or strain. His resurrection is dripping with grace as much as it is with glorious new possibility.

The patient grace with which Jesus lived his transformation is a model for how we may live ours. In a culture characterized by doing as much as we can as fast as we can, to the point of stressing out ourselves and those around us, how soul-easing it is to know that personal transformation can have as much patience and grace in it as challenge. Change filled with grace is in the spirit of the words attributed to Jesus in Matthew 11:28-29:

> *Come to me, all you that are carrying heavy burdens, and I will give you rest. Take my yoke upon you and learn from me, for I am gentle and humble in heart, and you will find rest in your souls.*

Paul reflects this notion of change at the pace of grace when he encourages us in Romans 6:4 not to sprint or strive in the newness of life, but to "walk in the newness of life." As we walk in the newness of life, we are more likely to stick to our transformation, to be less demanding and judgmental of ourselves and others, and to savor and enjoy the change process as much as the change result.

If we are willing, God is willing to transform us at the pace of grace. And God's grace is no small matter.

Just as we are is always good enough for God's grace.

In the light of God's grace there is constant sacred acceptance and celebration of you for who you are, not what you do.

Choosing To Be Raised

Though Jesus called Lazarus from the tomb, he didn't force him out. Lazarus had to choose to come forth.

Lazarus might have ignored the voice of Jesus and pretended not to hear it. I remember reading somewhere that "the hardest thing to do in life is to awaken someone who is only pretending to be asleep."

Secondly, Lazarus could have heard his name called, come out, and then gone right back into the tomb. After all, he had been dead long enough to have gotten used to being lifeless. Sometimes we choose to cling to the familiar simply because it is familiar, no matter how deadly it may be.

Finally, Lazarus might not have exited the tomb at all, afraid of the changes that awaited him with the onset of new life. Newness is fine for most of us, as long as it doesn't challenge us to change too much.

By not fully owning our power to choose, we conveniently relinquish responsibility for our reality. This allows us to blame God and others for what happens or doesn't happen in life.

Choosing is a gift. Let us receive it and the grace and the sacred responsibility that accompanies it.

SAYING YES TO A NEW VERSION OF YOURSELF

Edward Kennedy "Duke" Ellington has been called "the most prolific composer of the twentieth century in terms of number of compositions [an estimated 2000] and variety of forms." Among Ellington's most revered works are "Mood Indigo," "Sophisticated Lady," and the symphonic suites "Black, Brown, and Beige" and "Harlem." One of the highlights of Ellington's illustrious career was a series of Sacred Concerts about which he said, "I was able to say loudly and openly what I have been saying to myself on my knees."

Perhaps the secret to Ellington's astounding creativity was his thirst for newness. Jazz critic Stanley Crouch writes, "Ellington was unable to settle for an earlier version of himself." Author Albert Murray reflected that Ellington was blessed with an "experimental disposition."

Perhaps the best expression of Ellington's openness to newness comes from Ellington himself. When asked to identify his favorite composition Ellington's answer was always the same, "My next one."

Trust Your Way Through

There is meaning in waiting.

There will be someone or something

to help you at the trying places on your path.

Unseen ground is not unsure ground.

Discouragement still has courage in it.

There are marvelous hidden lessons

in the valley moments.

Take strength from the struggle,

and trust your way through.

CHAPTER 6

Grace Sparks: Using Words to Ignite New Life

§

*"Words are powerful when chosen well
and hurled with precision."*

--NNEDI OKORAFOR, THE BOOK OF PHOENIX

JOHN BEGINS HIS GOSPEL BY heralding that Jesus was with God in the beginning as the "Word of God," imagining and creating the world. Is it no wonder that words are as powerful as they are?

Think of a time when something you said or heard made a transformative difference in your life. Words have the power to urge us on and hold us back. What we say matters--especially what we say to ourselves.

As living manifestations of the breath of God ourselves, it is in us to daily co-create our reality with God by the things we believe and say. The truth is, we are doing this all the time. For instance when we mindlessly decry the weather, we posture ourselves for a down day. The question is, will you choose to mindlessly think and say things that diminish your experience, or become a conscious and positive co-creator with God, by continually thinking and speaking life- enhancing reality. Should you choose to, you may speak new life any time you wish.

I call forth new life daily through *Grace Sparks. Grace Sparks* are short reflections that I use to encourage, enlighten, and energize my spirit—to spark and cultivate my awareness and ability as a child of God. I share one or two grace sparks each day on Facebook at "Yes to Grace." All you have to do is "like" the page, and you'll start receiving them. I have also published a collection of 100 Grace Sparks, with more collections and Apps to come in the future. Here are 70 brand new *Grace Sparks*:

1

Gratitude Inspires Attitude.

An Inspired Attitude Enhances Perception.

An Enhanced Perception Unleashes New Possibilities.

2

Your sacred self-esteem, unique vision, and creative courage matter.

Stop hiding your flame.

3

If you can trust that God hears you,

you can make it, no matter what else you hear.

4

To always be curious about something is to

constantly make God smile.

5

May you be so filled with gratitude and curiosity

that bitterness and discouragement always feel too cramped to stay.

6

There is no charge to be new each day:

Notice

Explore

Wonder

7

Look a great trial in the face until it softens,

and whispers a secret strength you never knew you had.

8

To be deeply interested in life is to be a

co-conspirator with God in daily amazement.

9

Delightfully tend to your inspirations;

they are God's way of delightfully tending to you.

10

Daily awareness and appreciation is the highest form of praise.

11

When you would give up, give in to God's tenacious grace.

12

No matter where we are,

we are never outside of God's elegant grace.

13

Tending to our wounds helps to keep us from

wounding others and ourselves unknowingly.

14

Don't let unattended wounds keep you from unusual healing.

15

No matter how it appears or feels,

nothing in our lives ever occurs

outside the reach and watch of God.

Our task is to remain ever open

to God's relentless grace

that never gives out

and never gives up.

16

*What if the divine will you seek is hidden in your recurring soulful
desires?*

Listen to your lingering longings.

17

The ultimate healing for rejection is God's grace.

18

Accepting our divine acceptance frees us to flow with unconditional love.

19

Refreshed by grace and lifted by love,

dare to face whatever is before you

with fabulous confidence.

20

We need not always struggle through change;

it is possible to dance transformation.

21

To live in the Spirit is to hear the rhythms of new possibilities

and not be afraid to play along.

22

The day would not mind if you intentionally took your time,

and delighted your way through it.

23

Grace Delight:

Suddenly finding

what you never knew

you were searching for.

24

Your solitude is a gift to the world.

The secretly enriched soul enriches us all.

25

Heaven sees little difference between a disciple at prayer,

a student at study, and a child at play.

26

To have special persons and moments, long gone,

suddenly appear in your mind, is to have the

past behold you with marvel, and wave you on.

27

Grace doesn't mind when we clarify, prioritize, plan, and execute.

Grace and grit dance well together.

28

There is an Insistent Love that sits with the broken,

and says not a word

as it begins its silent mending.

29

Sometimes it's not that words are not enough, it's that they are too much.

Enter music and stillness.

30

When it comes to space, time, and lightness of heart, be generous with yourself.

31

A voice whispered, "Come, let me show you how to walk on water.

It's not about what's under your feet;

it's about what's in your heart."

32

What a precious revelation it is to finally recognize a secret grace,

that has been helping you to make it through, all this time.

33

Keep your life fresh by being newly unknowing: filled with curiosity and humility,

and easily delighted.

34

God does not force us to be inspired.

It is our choice to notice inspirations and ride like the wind.

35

May you be so busy being amazed that you have little time to be afraid.

36

Learning to be content without being complacent is golden.

Contentment is peace poised for transformation.

37

Prayer is a holy playground where we explore new possibilities

and catch visions beyond our expectations.

38

Expect to be refreshed.

39

If you can sense the royalty in yourself,

you can spot the royalty in others.

40

Sometimes God writes upside down just to get us to see things from a different perspective.

41

There is an unusual sacred flow that comes with being

Focused,

Lighthearted,

Open,

and Willing.

42

Dear Beloved,

Be loved.

Be love.

Be.

43

Go in Grace.

Step in Peace.

Walk in Love.

Just trust that God is with you,

and you will always have

just the strength you need.

44

The sun does not hesitate to shine, and neither should you.

45

We cannot walk into our fulfillment by only listening to familiar sounds.

Stay ever alert for what you have never heard before.

46

Take heart; you are always more than you presently know yourself to be.

47

I claim my limitless inner sacred abundance, and live from wealth—not for wealth.

48

Still waters bear wonder.

Pay attention to what you hear when your mind is at ease.

49

There is sacred living water within you that always glistens with new life.

50

Be on the look-out for "back alley blessings": hidden

benefits from situations that threaten to break your spirit.

51

Remain watchful for diamonds on detours.

52

May your childlike wonder never grow up.

53

God has an even better blessing behind the one you are praying for.

54

A leaf declared in mid air,
"I'm not falling; I'm flying!"
How you see it determines
how you live it.

55

Question: What good is all the love in the world if we don't believe in it?
Answer: All the love in the world believing in us.

56

What if

the wild rumor
is true

that God was caught

dancing in you?

57

Gladly open the gift of being gentle with yourself.

58

When the Spirit

gives you the green light,

go

with all your might.

59

Dare to walk in your wonderful.

60

To inspire and to be inspired is to taste heaven.

61

To always be curious about something is to

always be making God smile.

62

Your highest praise to God is you.

63

Just because it's still hurting doesn't mean

the healing hasn't started.

64

Sometimes, the evening breeze is strong enough to blow away every fear.

65

One way to find your calling is to notice those things

you get lost in.

66

When playing hide-and-seek,

gratitude always knows where to find joy.

67

Receive Grace; Take Your Time; Have Fun!

68

To be easily delighted is an unsung gift of the spirit.

69

Grace is God's endless love letter to you.

70

Fall in love with your transformation.

Epilogue

§

New Life is No Joke—and The Best Laugh of All!
Because God never stops being God, new life is always in the air.
This means we may be renewed each day, many times a day.
God delightfully dares you to receive daily renewing.
Take the divine dare.
Call forth new life.
Imagine and become your freshest, finest, and fullest self!

Don't Just Read About Calling Forth New Life; Do It!

Calling Forth New Life: The In-Visioning Journal

Receive Brand New Grace Sparks

Each Day at

"Yes to Grace"

on Facebook!

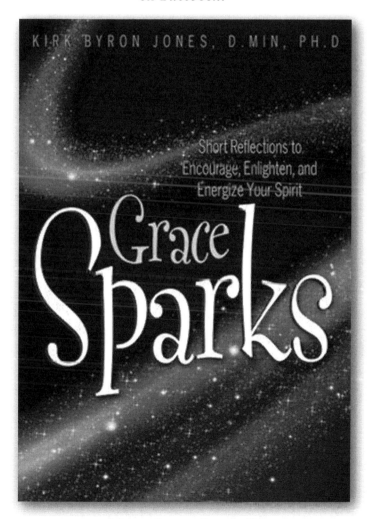

More Grace Sparks!!

About the Author

BORN IN NEW ORLEANS, LOUISIANA, as the second son to the late Frederick and Ora Mae Jones, Kirk Byron Jones is a graduate of Loyola University and Andover Newton Theological School, and holds a Doctor of Ministry degree from Emory University and a Doctor of Philosophy degree from Drew University.

Dr. Jones began preaching at age 12, and has served as a pastor for over thirty years. He was the founding minister of Beacon Light Baptist Church in New Orleans, and Senior Minister at Calvary Baptist Church, Chester, PA; Ebenezer Baptist Church, Boston, MA; and the First Baptist Churches of Randolph and Tewksbury MA. He presently serves as Senior Pastor of Zion Baptist Church in

Lynn, Massachusetts. Throughout his pastoral ministry, Rev. Jones has served on various religious and civic committees at the local and national level.

A professor for over twenty-five years, Dr. Jones has served as Director of the Kelsey-Owens Black Ministries Program and Kelsey-Owens Professor at Andover Newton Theological School. Currently an adjunct professor of social ethics, preaching, and pastoral ministry at Andover Newton Theological School, Dr. Jones serves as guest preacher and teacher at churches, schools and conferences throughout the United States. His writings have been published in various journals, including *The Christian Century, Leadership, Gospel Today, Pulpit Digest,* and *The African American Pulpit,* a quarterly preaching journal he co-founded in 1997.

Dr. Jones is the author of several best-selling books for clergy, and all persons seeking spiritual growth in a changing and challenging world. His books include the following titles:

Rest in the Storm: Self-Care Strategies for Clergy and Other Caregivers

Addicted to Hurry: Spiritual Strategies for Slowing Down

The Jazz of Preaching: How to Preach with Great Freedom and Joy

Morning B.R.E.W.: A Divine Power Drink for Your Soul

The Morning B.R.E.W. Journal

Holy Play: The Joyful Adventure of Unleashing Your Divine Purpose

Say Yes to Grace: How to Burn Bright Without Burning Out

The Sacred Seven: How to Create, Manage, and Sustain a Fulfilling Life

Fulfilled: Living and Leading with Unusual Wisdom, Peace, and Joy

Refill: Meditations for Leading with Wisdom, Peace, and Joy

Grace Sparks: Short Reflections to Encourage, Enlighten, and Energize Your Spirit

His latest book is entitled, *Calling Forth New Life: Becoming Your Freshest, Finest, and Fullest Self.*

Dr. Jones is the creator/author of the Facebook page "Yes to Grace" where he offers brief inspirational messages in words and images. Currently, "Yes to Grace" has over 80,000 subscribers. For more information about his writing and teaching ministry, you may visit www.kirkbjones.com.

Dr. Jones is married to Mary Brown-Jones. They have 4 adult children, 3 grandchildren, and reside in Randolph, MA. When not engaged in the holy play of his labor, he enjoys leisurely fun, most especially, listening to jazz, reading, journaling, and playing video games.

THANK YOU FOR READING MY OFFERING.

I WOULD APPRECIATE YOUR TAKING A MOMENT TO POST A REVIEW ON AMAZON. COM

HAPPY NEW LIFE!